Quixote Contemplates Retirement

Quixote Contemplates Retirement

Poems by

Lew Maltby

Cover design by Shay Culligan
Cover image by iStock Photo
Author image by Robert Radner

ISBN: 978-1-63980-510-5

Kelsay Books
502 South 1040 East, A-119
American Fork, Utah 84003
Kelsaybooks.com

To Aaron, Julia, and Ellie

Acknowledgments

Thank you to the following publications, where versions of these poems previously appeared:

Barzakh Poetry Journal: "Mr. Public Defender" (as "Mr. P.D.")

U.S. 1 Worksheets: "D'Jemma el Fna," "I Call Her Sunshine," "Ulysses in Love," "Weekend Warriors"

Contents

Mr. Public Defender

In the halls of justice, justice is in the halls

Knight errant in a cheap suit
butt-sniffing the black robed gargoyle
perched upon the bench, a bad actor

pretending to believe
the blue perjury parade.
Defendants plead

"not guilty"
as if it mattered,
not in on the joke.

I serve him up an easy one
kid caught hot-wiring a car
first offense.

He slams it into the upper deck,
a year in Holmesburg.
(Didn't he get the memo?)

Suddenly a sorcerer,
I conjure missing files
and unavailable witnesses

with dazzling ease, the tide
of perjury turning
until the clock runs out.

Just another punch-
card day in the justice factory,
floors slippery with invisible blood.

Boomers

Greatest generation's joy
and pride, gnaw out of suburban cocoons,

discover evil for the thousandth
first time, rushing home with our discovery like a
straight-A report card,

refuse Uncle Lyndon's game of dominos,
throw flowers at the monster tilting
at tanks with paper lances.

Carefree puppies playing in the gun barrel
of history until four shrouded messengers
from Ohio reveal our parents' true first love.

After Ozymandias

. . . and sneer of cold command . . .
—Percy Bysshe Shelley, "Ozymandias"

He came from Bradford
black hole in Pennsylvania north woods
a genie escaping from the bottle

hurtling through the world deaf and brutal
as a stone, commanding pinstriped
legions, leaving wreckage in his wake.

I dodged arrest at seventeen
more afraid of him than the police.
The judge who years later locked me up for contempt of court
a mere pussycat.

Once a professional poker shark.
Now he plays cards with my daughter.
They stick to blackjack. The math is easier.

Terrifying inspiration, ghost
of Christmas yet to come
from which no good deed can save me.

Mildred

Mom was quieter than the rest of us,
shorter too.

Reliable mouse
bringing grape juice ice cube tributes
to measled royalty,
seeking acceptance with the currency
of service,

standing at the playground gate
waiting for an invitation
to live,
hopes curdling,

passing through the world without leaving
a shadow.

Weekend Warriors

Valkyries in ponytails
streak across the green,
ball-seeking missiles of boisterous mayhem
giving everything for nothing
in a sisterhood of sweat.

After the whistle,
bloodlust morphs to bonhomie
in a sea of warm beer.
Warriors retreat to the library
to battle with Proust

on a winesap afternoon
high above the Hudson.

I Call Her Sunshine

Leatherneck nurses,
bright eyes stolen by seeing too much, hard
as the potholed streets of Trenton,
called our baby “the angel.”
Born in a battleship gray health factory
she emerged from the section’s maw,
bloody as a boxer in the 15th round,
smiling at the doctor,
as he struck the world’s first blow.

For Julia

Wild pony on spindly legs,
    chasing nameless horizons.

Irresistible force in search of immovable objects
    fleeing the abyss of ordinary.

When you break the tape and win the ribbon,
    will the color match your eyes?

Marlin

Eight miles off Mombasa,
blue lightning strikes in green water.
Banshee shriek of line,
recaptured inch by sweat-stained inch.

Silver torpedo erupts,
etching watery lace against the sky.

Endless tug of war.
Momentary triumph.

Captive's blank-eyed stare,
I count coup, cut the line to change partners
and begin the dance again.

D'Jemma el Fna

Marrakech

To reach "place of the apocalypse"
tumble into any rabbit hole,
dog shit and broken glass,
dodge pinball motorbike boys,
follow the sweet stew of jasmine
and muezzin wolf howls
to a towerless Babel
where saffron sun assaults,
sleepy camels wander,
hawk-eyed men with cobras
drift you eyeless
toward the point of no return.

Hopefully Not Icarus

Only bird shit and fools fall from the sky
—82nd Airborne

Standing in a black puddle
of fear, 3,000 feet above a doll house landscape,
drop zone a treeless dot below.

I finger the rosary
arithmetic of safety.

Behind me, beautiful Genevieve,
excited as a puppy, won't be
impressed if I wet my pants.

Tap on the shoulder—my turn.
Step blind into a whoosh
of dark tunnel.

Emerge a milkweed in timeless blue.

Contra Dancing

Float lost
in a bubble of sound,
heartbeat synced to band rhythms.
Defy the tyranny of gravity.

Hawk-spiral
endlessly upward.

Dervish-seek.
Escape velocity.

Skyrocket-ache
to explode

until the bubble bursts
and I walk again on broken knees.

Tantalus

. . . a man's reach should exceed his grasp,
Or what's a heaven for?
—Robert Browning, "Andrea del Sarto"

Sorrel mustang leaps ever beyond rope's reach.
Perfect melody with one eternal flat note.
Rainbow's disdain for angler's earnest fly.
Sculpture wandering lost in oaken block.
Winning touchdown pass six inches from hungry fingertips.
It's a poet's life.
Get used to it.

Lady and the Tramp

She offers Fabergé eggs
clever fingers spinning words into gold.

I drag in stumps
    ripped from earth like bad teeth
    shaped with a chain saw.

Great bloody slabs of raw meat,
    heart still beating.

Some Choose Flowers

Some write flowers.
I choose blood.
Nothing against flowers.
I feel their ache as beauty fades.
But flowers do not quicken
my pulse, make me
forget my name and
set myself on fire.

Haiku

Red and gold leaf
sails on winter wind.
How quietly it falls.

Bear Baiting

I.

Naked in her bed,
a bear in a pit,
I exchange knowing glances with the mob

II.

Escaping into the black swamp of her body,
on sails of Spanish moss,
I sink into a mangrove nest,
cinch tight my cloak of silt,
draw dark water through my gills

Leap of Faith

Standing
at the precipice—

Gazing
into the black hole
of her eyes—

Leaning
into the yearning—

diving
jubilant
into the abyss—

’Til

the babbling brook takes a vow
of silence and nattering nabobs
of negativism look on
the bright side—

’Til dangling participles get
a grip, and pregnant pauses join
the PTA—

’Til the “gets” are all got
and all the swashes buckled—

’Til we know who wrote the book of love
and what Julio was doing down by the schoolyard—

I’ll be the robocall you can’t escape,
the burr on your hiking shorts,
the cool spot on your pillow.

Ulysses in Love

Blue-eyed sailor
  adrift on a sea of moon-white skin,

I follow familiar contours
  of hip and thigh

toward the salty tang
  of mangrove,

drink the sirens' song
  with naked ears,

travel song lines past the dragon's border

seeking safe harbor
  in the storm's eye.

Words Fail Me

Apologies to Ogden Nash

I love you more than I hate going bald,
though that's really not so bad.

I love you more than I miss the years together
we never had.

I love you more than *Giant Steps*
and chocolate ice cream, too.

More than my red bike when I was twelve
and it was new.

I love you more than Donald Trump
hates the ACLU.

I wanted to write something so deep and true
it would bring tears to your eyes.
But honey,

I can't find the words for my love for you,
so I had to try being funny.

How Much Did You Love Me?

More than you knew,
less than I thought.

Suspended Animation

Sleepwalk through another sled-dog day
of deafening silence in the half light
of a discouraged sun,
limping across the sky like a three-legged dog,

stare at an empty canvas, search for a reason
to pick up a brush.

Turn to the news to watch the odometer of death.

Mark the time on gilded cell walls,
every lost day a small victory.

If I were Rip Van Winkle
I would set the alarm for half-past March.

Ring Around the Rosy

Once we were lords,
masters of all we surveyed.

Now, headless chickens
under a falling sky
as the long-hidden worm
emerges from the apple.

Cowering in our castles, drawbridge up,
loved ones reduced to electrons on a screen
we stare into website tea leaves
to divine our fate,

venture out timidly,
behind flimsy cotton armor,
shadow box with death,
giving up life to continue living.

Stranger in a Strange Land

I believe it because it is absurd
—Tertullian

Remember when Walter Cronkite tucked the country into bed
each night and we all knew how it was?

When outlaws wore masks
and boring Republicrats minded the store?

Before the flaming organ grinder
made monkeys dance
and tweeting in tongues our lingua franca.

When did sanity go AWOL?
Cat burglar slipping stealthy out the back door
leaving us lost in the not-so-funhouse.

When did the answer to every question become a snarling dog?

Quixote Contemplates Retirement

A man's got to know his limitations.
—Dirty Harry Callahan, *Magnum Force*

Graying crusader,
self-appointed injustice junkie
still searching for Archimedes' platform
to move a stubborn world—

surveys a legacy of ink stains
and momentary disturbances of molecular air.

Aborted heads of monsters that might have been
adorn the wall, visible only to me,
a parade of counterfactuals.

Damsels waltz by, oblivious to dodged bullets
of distress, lonely pocket, no gold watch.

Let someone else slay the next dragon.

About the Author

Lew Maltby has been a factory worker, trial lawyer, truck driver, soldier, and corporate executive. He wrote his first poem at 35. Urged by friends, he submitted it to the North Dakota State poetry competition and was amazed when he won.

Lew finds poetry in unlikely places—tracer bullets over his head, the call of hyenas in the African night, the snarl of chainsaws, prostitutes staggering home at 5 AM.

From 2020 to 2023, he was managing editor of *U.S. 1 Worksheets.*

His poems have appeared In *Stillwater Review, River Poet's Journal, Moonstone Press,* and *U.S. 1 Worksheets.* Kelsay Books published his first chapbook, *Smiling Axes,* in 2019.

www.ingramcontent.com/pod-product-compliance
Lightning Source LLC
LaVergne TN
LVHW010549100826
845148LV00013B/2664
* 9 7 8 1 6 3 9 8 0 5 1 0 5 *